AWFULLY ANCIENT

LOOS, POOS and Number Twos

A disgusting journey
through the
bowels of history!

First published in 2014 by Wayland

Copyright © Wayland 2014

Wayland
338 Euston Road
London
NW1 3BH

Wayland Australia
Level 17/207 Kent Street
Sydney NSW 2000

Senior editor: Julia Adams
Illustrator: Tom Morgan-Jones
Designer: Rocket Design (East Anglia) Ltd

Dewey classification: 392.3'6-dc23

ISBN 978 0 7502 7986 4
E-book ISBN 978 0 7502 8822 4

Printed in China
10 9 8 7 6 5 4 3 2 1

Wayland is a division of Hachette Children's
Books, an Hachette UK company.
www.hachette.co.uk

This book is 'brimming' with poo and wee, so we thought we'd get stuck right in on this page with a steaming bucket of poo. Turn to page 22 to find out more...

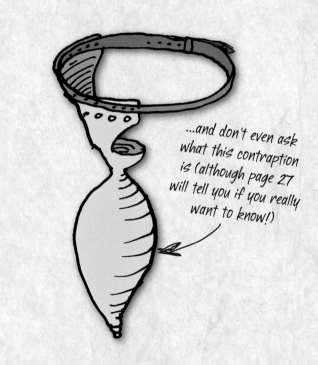

...and don't even ask what this contraption is (although page 27 will tell you if you really want to know!)

A bum sponge

Contents

Oh, the dreaded type 6...

Phew, somebody really HAS got a problem with that lot!

Wasn't me!

Funny how lots of people are shy when they talk about... erm... er... doing their business... er, you know, *going to the toilet*. So we're going to boldly introduce this great topic by looking straight down the pan with some excellent words.

Let's get them out in the open in alphabetical order: defecate, dung, excrement, faeces, manure, number twos, plop, poo, urine, wee wee. Go on shout a couple out loud; you know you want to. That's better. Now we can be serious.

History isn't just about kings, queens, battles and dates, history is about everyday things too. And most people have to urinate and defecate every day. The greatest emperors and the humblest peasants had to poop and wee. Even your teacher has to poop. (Yeah, we know some probably don't, but that's because teachers aren't really human.)

How much you poop depends on your sex, age and what you have eaten, but a good estimate for an adult male is 500 grams a day. Multiply that by, let's say, 10,000 people for a year. Now you have one of the great problems of human civilisation: sanitation. People's faeces may carry harmful organisms and many diseases are spread by contact with faeces. That's what makes loos and poos such a great topic for historians.

Old Viking Proverb:
Everyone loves the smell of their own farts. Bet you do too.

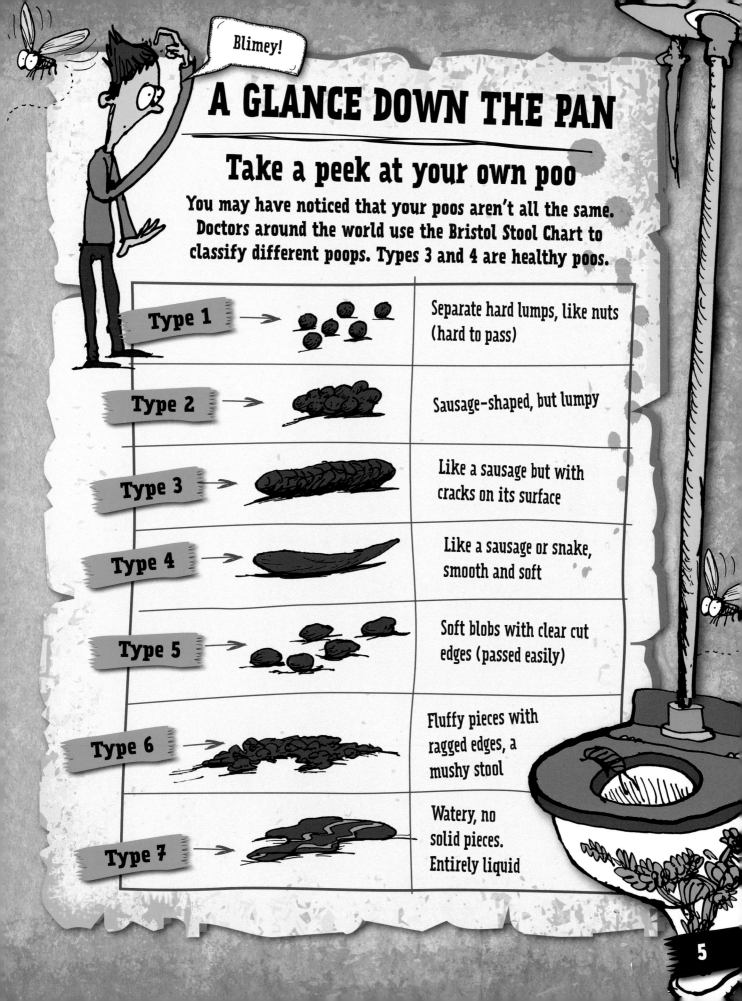

Blimey!

A GLANCE DOWN THE PAN

Take a peek at your own poo

You may have noticed that your poos aren't all the same.
Doctors around the world use the Bristol Stool Chart to
classify different poops. Types 3 and 4 are healthy poos.

Type 1 →		Separate hard lumps, like nuts (hard to pass)
Type 2 →		Sausage-shaped, but lumpy
Type 3 →		Like a sausage but with cracks on its surface
Type 4 →		Like a sausage or snake, smooth and soft
Type 5 →		Soft blobs with clear cut edges (passed easily)
Type 6 →		Fluffy pieces with ragged edges, a mushy stool
Type 7 →		Watery, no solid pieces. Entirely liquid

Ancient Loos and Poos

Dinosaur Dumps

In 2013, the world's oldest 'public toilet' was found by palaeontologists in Argentina. It was used as a vast dumping ground by a 2.4-metre-long herbivore called Dinodontosaurus, 240 million years ago.

Give that five minutes!

New poo may be a problem, but old poo is an archaeologist's dream. Fossilised faeces, or dry dung, are called coprolites, and are the best evidence about the diet and health of past peoples and animals.

Predator poop

In 2009, archaeologists in South Africa found evidence of the dangers early humans faced from predators. The oldest known human hair (around 200,000 years old) was found in a 24.8 centimetre block of hyena dung. So we could say instead of 'blood on its paws' the hyena was caught with 'hair in its poop'!

Oi! Bag it!

Poo changes history

So far, the oldest human droppings found go back 18,000 years, and were discovered in Wadi Kuabbaniya in southern Egypt. However, the USA is in the race, too. In 2002–3, 14 ancient coprolites were found in the Paisley Caves in Oregon, and they changed American history.

The poop is around 14,300 years old, which pushed back evidence of human settlement in North America by 1,000 years. DNA tests suggest the poopers were hunters and had recently eaten red fox, coyote or wolf, or that these animals had peed on the poo after the humans left.

A GLANCE DOWN THE PAN

Ancient loo show-down

Archaeologists keep hunting for the oldest loo.
Here's a list of five top (or should that be bottom?) finds:

Place	Date	Loo Info
Skara Brae on the Bay of Skaill, Orkney	3000 BCE	A settlement of eight houses, each with an indoor loo and drain
Palace of Knossos, Crete	1900–1100 BCE	A sewerage system made from clay pipes and loos flushed by rainwater
Rach Nui, Long An Province, Vietnam	1500–2000 BCE	A latrine pit with perfectly preserved poo
Cavustepe Fortress, Turkey	764–735 BCE	The oldest surviving squat toilet, probably used by King Sardur II
Henan Province, China	Han Dynasty 206 BCE–24 CE	A loo in a royal tomb ready for use in the afterlife. Flushed by piped water, with a seat and an arm rest.

Dried Poos and Worms!

Loos and Poos in Ancient Egypt

Bedtime read

The most famous Egyptian medical 'textbook' is the Ebers Papyrus, a scroll about 20 metres long, written in around 1600 BCE.

Think Egyptians and we think big construction projects, such as the pyramids. Building these vast monuments meant thousands of workers living in makeshift towns for years — and a huge poo problem.

'Hygienic' poo

To stop diseases ripping through the workforce, workers ate plenty of radishes, garlic and onions, foods full of chemicals effective against diseases such as dysentery. In permanent settlements, most people just found a private pooping spot or went to the village latrine area and pooped there. This doesn't sound great but Egypt is, and was, a very hot country so the poop dried quickly and became less of a health hazard.

Poop canal

Ahhhhh...

Uh oh...

Garlic helped combat poo-related illnesses...

A GLANCE DOWN THE PAN

Poo is good for you

Egyptian doctors used so much animal and human poo in spells and remedies that archaeologists have nicknamed these cures 'sewage pharmacology'.

- **Cure for a splinter:** soak in a mixture of worms' blood and donkey poo.

- **Cure for swollen eyes:** rub on cattle pee and pigs gall (bile).

- **Cure for lesions of the skin:** After the scab has fallen off, put on a poultice made with scribe's poo and fresh milk.

- **Cure for a wound:** make a poultice with human poo, yeast of sweet beer and honey.

But before we fall about laughing, chemists have found germ-killing substances in some of the popular ingredients of Egyptian medicine, such as myrrh, yeast, honey, mud, and animal liver.

Poop canals

More of a problem was people pooping in the irrigation canals that ran close to most settlements. These were also used for drinking water, bathing, washing clothes and as splash pools for kids. Diarrhoea, caught from water contaminated by faeces, led to the deaths of about one in three young children.

Rich people had bathrooms in their homes, but the toilet was often just a large pot sunk into the floor or drained to the outside by clay, stone or metal pipes. The poop either soaked into the ground or was taken away by a slave or servant.

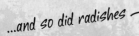
...and so did radishes

9

Hysterical Hygiene!

Loos and Poos in Ancient Greece

That's Hygeia, the goddess of cleanliness

You can blame the Greeks for the word hygiene. Asclepius was the Greek god of medicine, and his daughter was Hygeia, goddess of cleanliness. It was just as well she was there to help, because the Greeks weren't great on sanitation.

Dirty streets

Greek towns were among the most sophisticated in the ancient world with market places, graceful temples and brilliant sports facilities, but most didn't have sewage systems. According to the writer Aristophanes (about 446–386 BCE), men relieved themselves in the street, wherever they happened to be.

The Greeks liked to keep clean and many houses and bathrooms had washstands and hip baths to sit down in. However, the toilets were just chamber pots. These were clay vessels that could be carried and emptied in the streets.

Storm sewers

The greatest Greek city, Athens, was a little better. The Athenians drew their water from springs near the Acropolis and from fountains supplied by underground aqueducts. There was a sewerage system in the city centre. This was known as the Great Drain and was washed clean when rain storms hit.

Storm water swept the wee and poo into a collection basin outside the city; it then flowed through brick lined conduits to fertilise nearby fields and orchards. Nevertheless, the famous doctor Hippocrates recognised the risks of water pollution and advised boiling water before consuming it to remove poisons.

Public poops

The Greeks had public loos in bath houses and gymnasiums, but there were no private stalls. The poet Antiphanes commented, 'If you think you are better than everyone else, going to the public latrine will put you in your place.'

A GLANCE DOWN THE PAN
Potty Greeks

The Agora Museum in Athens has a potty training chair that's 2,600 years old. The hole at the front was probably to let smells out and make it easier to clean. It looks difficult to get out of, too – just the place to stick an annoying little brother or sister!

Public Pooping

Loos and Poos in Ancient Rome

A posh Roman loo

SNACK BAR

GYM

That's obviously one of yours Brian, so don't try denying it!

Rome was the greatest city in the ancient world and the centre of a mighty empire. In 100 CE, when the population of Londinium (today's London) was around 60,000, more than one million people lived in Rome. So there was a whole lot of pooping going on.

Fresh water

The Roman water supply was pretty good. Nine aqueducts, with a total length of 422 km, carried clean water from the Apennine Mountains to the city. Over one billion litres reached Rome every day and flowed to fountains and cisterns, where people filled their water jars.

Spa time

Most Romans lived in crowded multi-storey blocks of flats, called *insula*. Only the very best had toilets or a water supply.

Flying poo

Rather than wash or poo in their small apartments, Romans went to public baths called *thermae*. There were more than 900 baths to choose from and some were amazing. The Baths of Diocletian, opened in 306 CE, had facilities for 3,000 people and included hot and cold pools, gyms, snack bars and a library.

Public pooping

Most public toilets were at the baths and were flushed with waste water from the pools. Bottoms were wiped with sponges that were thrown away.

A common complaint about the baths was lazy people pooping or peeing in the water — instead of popping to the loo.

Wee smile

The Romans used wee for whitening their teeth. Wee is full of the chemical ammonia, a strong cleaner.

A bum sponge

At night, Romans used chamber pots in their flats

A GLANCE DOWN THE PAN
The flying poo problem

At night, Romans used chamber pots in their flats – and some tenement blocks were five or six stories high... Bet you've worked it out.

Rather than walk up and down dozens of steps, the pots were emptied – or even the whole pot thrown – into the street.

The problem was so bad, a law was brought in: the *Dejecti Effusive Actio*. Anyone hit by flying poo or pots could claim compensation.

A bit more flying poo!

Beware the Purple Goddess

Loos and Poos in Ancient China

Anyone fancy a basket of poo?

The ancient Chinese were very practical about poo. They used animal dung as fertiliser for their crops; however, the amount of animal poop wasn't enough, so they came up with a rather smart idea...

People power

In order to make up for the lack of animal dung, human poo was collected and used for fertiliser. No farmer was too proud to carry a basket of turds to the fields, though it was often women's work. Guests were invited to use the loo and add their valuable poop to the pile.

Pigs and poos

Many toilets were pig latrines: an outhouse mounted over a pig sty with a hole to drop the poo to the pigs. Pigs eat almost anything organic, and find human poo quite tasty.

Quick, get it while it's warm.

Express delivery!

Imagine using bamboo strips or broken pottery – that's a real BUM DEAL!

A GLANCE DOWN THE PAN
Invention of toilet paper *(hooray!)*

Traditionally, wealthy Chinese people wiped their bottoms with waste silk while the poor scraped their bums with bamboo strips and broken pottery. **Ouch!**

The Chinese invented paper around 100 CE and by the ninth century, toilet paper was big business. In 1393, Emperor Hongwu's imperial family used 15,000 sheets of specially made soft, perfumed paper.

Soft and scented

Models of pigs' loos from the Han dynasty (206 BCE to 220 CE) have been found in tombs — ready for pooping on the pigs in the next life.

Lady of the lavatory

The ancient Chinese even had a toilet goddess! The tale goes: In the fifth century CE, the jealous first wife of a government official murdered his younger, second wife by shoving her into a toilet pit. The Ruler of Heaven took pity on the poor woman and, because of her horrible death, made her The Violet Lady, goddess of the toilet.

Incantation to the Violet Lady

To be said on the 15th day of the first month of the Chinese New Year:

Your husband is not at home and his first wife has gone out. So, little damsel, you may come out.

Try that at home and freak your family out.

Poo Chutes and Piss Pots

Loos and Poos in medieval times

Gong

Gong was a medieval word for a toilet or its contents. Try it at school: 'Got to go to the gong for a gong, Miss.'

Gongfermor

Medieval towns were grim. London in the fourteenth century had a population of 100,000 people, but only eight public toilets. Many streets had no sewers and those that did were open drains – ditches running down the street. Often they were blocked and stinking.

Cleaning up

After the Black Death wiped out around a third of Londoners, the city tried to deal with some of the mess:

Muckrakers were the first street cleaners. They cleared up the piles of poo and other delights such as offal from butchers' shops and moved it by cart or boat outside the city walls.

A GLANCE DOWN THE PAN
Crusading worms

Knights on the Crusades used the island of Cyprus as a base and left behind a treat for archaeologists – 30 years' worth of dried poo in a latrine at Castle Saranda Kolones.

The rehydrated faeces were full of the eggs of giant roundworms, parasites that live in the guts of humans. The parasites siphoned off nutrients from food the Crusaders ate, leaving them suffering from malnutrition.

Eww, gross!

Gongfermors cleaned out cesspits, latrines and privies. A perk of the job was selling the waste to farmers around London.

Garderobes and reredorters

Castles had lavatories, called *garderobes* or privies. They were set into the thick walls with shoots to drop the poo into the moat. The name *garderobe* means guarding robes or clothes. This may have come from the practice of hanging clothes in the toilet shaft so the ammonia from the urine would kill fleas or moths.

Monasteries built the best loos in the Middle Ages. Toilets for monks were called the *reredorter* and were usually built over or flushed by a nearby river. The monks spent many hours praying, so they used piss pots, peeing discretely under their robes.

The word 'loo' dates from medieval times. When people with full chamber pots emptied them in the street, they yelled a warning: *gardez l'eau!* (pronounced 'gardezloo') — watch out for the water! Gardez l'eau became loo.

Gardez l'eau!

What the...

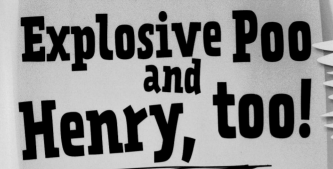

Explosive Poo and Henry, too!

Loos and Poos in Tudor times

Ah, the smell of wee...

Tudor king Henry VIII loved wars, and during his reign demand for gunpowder soared. When his forces invaded France in 1513, they carried 510 tons of gunpowder. The siege guns consumed 32 tons a day. You may now be asking yourself what this has to do with poo...

Poo saves the nation

Gunpowder is made from sulphur, charcoal and saltpetre. You already know that wee and poo make good fertiliser — and the same chemicals help make saltpetre. White saltpetre crystals grew in dry soil enriched with human or animal poo and wee — places such as barns, cellars, dovecotes, stables, old middens and dried out cesspits.

In Tudor times saltpetremen, licensed by the King, scoured the country and seized saltpetre wherever they could find it — whether the owners of the property liked it or not.

Pooping, Tudor style

The homes of wealthy Tudor families had privies built outside the main house. To save a walk in the cold, Tudor gentlemen often peed in the fireplace while ladies retired to a closet, a small room with a piss pot.

Henry VIII's palace at Hampton Court had a 'great house of easement': a double-decked latrine with 28 seats. It emptied into brick-lined drains, which carried the waste into the River Thames. The royal loos were cleaned by teams of young *gongfermors* — boys small enough to crawl along the drains.

A poo-powered siege gun

A GLANCE DOWN THE PAN
Groom of the stoole

Henry VIII used an impressive velvet-covered potty called a close stool. The courtier who emptied this – and wiped his bottom – was called the Groom of the Stoole. Far from being a bum job, this was a plum job. The Groom was the son of a nobleman and a trusted servant with a lot of influence.

The Great Stink

Poos in early Victorian times

Victorian towns stunk of... you guessed it: poo. In the hot summer of 1858 the stench from the River Thames was so intense that curtains soaked in chloride of lime were hung in Parliament to mask the smell. Even the Victorians called this The Great Stink. What had gone so wrong?

Poo pits

During the nineteenth century, cities across the globe exploded with people. Look at these amazing figures:

City	1800	1900
London	1,000,000	6,200,000
New York	80,000	3,500,000
Paris	50,000	2,700,000

As more and more migrants poured in, crowded city slums became death traps, with rampant epidemics of cholera and typhoid wiping out thousands. The cause was oodles of poop! Most ended up on midden heaps or in cesspits, but these leaked or overflowed, fouling streams and wells used for drinking water.

In London in 1841 health inspectors counted 3,000 cesspits and reckoned there were countless hidden ones. In New York in 1861, 60,000 cartloads of poo were scooped from cesspits and dumped off piers into the East River. In both cities, some posher homes

In Victorian times, the River Thames was a bit whiffy...

had water closets, but these were connected to storm drains and the faeces went straight in the nearest waterway.

The dreaded type 7. That's as bad as it gets, folks!

Nowhere to poop

With so few loos, poor families suffered most. Some pooped in the street and offended their wealthy neighbours, while others pooped in old newspapers and threw them outside. Most used chamber pots and emptied them in the street at night. In villages, homes kept piles of poop for fertiliser and wee in barrels to clean clothes.

A GLANCE DOWN THE PAN
Animal poo, too!

Victorian cities were full of animals. In 1876, **149,435 cows and bulls**, **1,659,324 sheep** and **14,394 pigs** walked through the streets of London to markets or slaughter houses. And yep – they pooped all the way. By 1900, 10 million tons of horse poo were cleared from English streets every year.

Victorians certainly needed to watch their step!

Toilet Revolution

Loos in Victorian Times

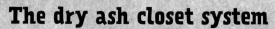

Poo pails were collected once a week – phaw!

After centuries of poo problems, it was the Victorians who finally came up with the solution. It's thanks to them that we don't have to poo in pits or buckets! But before the flushing loo graced bathrooms, a few other systems were trialled...

The pail system

Some towns bought thousands of buckets with lids (pails) and gave one to every household. They were emptied and disinfected once a week. In Edinburgh 14,000 houses had poo pails. Collection began at 6am and users were fined £2 (about £130 in today's money) if their pail wasn't out on time.

The dry ash closet system

Ash closets were better, but more expensive. Outside loos were built in yards. People still pooped into a big bucket under the toilet seat, but then they mixed ashes from the fire (every house had a coal fire) with the waste. This absorbed the liquid and some of the smell. The closets were emptied once a week by nightsoil men.

Towns recovered the cost by selling the poop to local famers. Nightsoil men in London sold cartloads of poo to famers for two shillings and sixpence (12.5p in today's money) until the 1870s. After this, cheap bird poop, called guano, was shipped in from South America to use as fertiliser, which put an end to the trade in human waste.

Take cover, it's a type 1!

Flushed with success

John Harrington invented the water closet during the reign of Elizabeth I, though it was never used. Joseph Bramah revived the idea of flush loos in the 1770s, but they were useless without a sewerage system. Enter London.

As soon as The Great Stink hit London, British Parliament passed a law to pay for new sewers for the capital. Between 1858 and 1865 a workforce of 6,000 people built 132 kilometres of brick sewers.

By 1900, most cities had sewerage systems and local laws made it compulsory for new houses to have flush toilets. It is very likely that your home town centre still uses Victorian sewers.

A GLANCE DOWN THE PAN

Paris first

The nation that led the way in sewerage systems was actually France. From 1852 to 1878, the brilliant engineer Eugene Belgrand built 600 kilometres of egouts (main sewers). We recommend the Musée des Égouts in Paris, which offers a sewer tour!

Toilet Tales

From the closet chronicles

White may not have been the best choice for the job...

Toilets and poop are part of everyday life, so they have played a crucial role in many historical events...

Murder on the loo

Murder 1: Sword and cesspit

Kings have to poop like everyone else, so quite a few have met their maker in a loo. In 1424, a gang of assassins came after James I of Scotland. To escape, he levered up the floor of the cesspit and hid in the stinking mess. It didn't save him. His killers jumped into the poop and ran him through with a sword.

Murder 2: Holy killer

In 1589, Henry III of France was holding court while seated on the royal chamber pot. This wasn't unusual; kings often pooped and talked at the same time. Henry was at war, so when a young monk claimed to have important papers, he was allowed to approach the King.

Big mistake, as the monk was a killer, and stabbed Henry in the gut.

White warriors

In the 1890s, the streets of New York were shin-deep in filth – human poo, horse poo, rotting food waste and dead animals. The situation was desperate. To tackle the emergency, veteran Civil War officer and sanitary engineer Colonel George Waring was put in charge of the Department of Street Cleaning, and ran it like an army.

Hundreds of men in WHITE uniforms, armed with brushes and shovels, cleared the streets. They started in the poorest areas, such as

That's a type 2 poo if I remember correctly?

Five Points, and even needed police protection. But within months the streets were clean.

Trench toilets

During the First World War (1914–18) millions of men sheltered in hundreds of kilometres of foul, muddy trenches. But even when bullets were flying, they still had to poop. Small latrine pits were dug off the main trench and fitted with a bucket, or even just a biscuit tin. Shovels of quick lime were thrown down to kill germs and the smell. Soldiers on sanitation duty risked their lives as they climbed out of the trenches to empty the buckets.

Going for a poop was dangerous as well. If enemy spotters picked out a latrine pit, they ordered an artillery strike — and targeted the privy!

Err, no thanks

Biscuit, sarge?

Toilet torture

Supporters of the twentieth-century Italian dictator Mussolini tortured opponents of his rule by forcing them to drink castor oil. This is a laxative and gave them explosive diarrhoea. Nasty!

Travelling Loos and Fast Poos

Wa-hey this is fun!

Pack it in, Ginger!

Violent manoeuvres in a Lancaster could cause a toilet disaster!

Planes

During the Second World War (1939–45) plane crews put up with primitive toilets. Fighter pilots had to unbutton their flight suit and pee into a relief bottle, while British Lancaster Bomber crews used portable on-board chemical toilets. However, if they were attacked and took evasive manoeuvres, the contents poured back into the plane.

American B17 bombers had relief tubes that drained wee outside, but it sprayed back over the bottom gun turret, and at high altitudes it froze to form a yellow cloud. The gunner couldn't see out; not ideal when German fighters were approaching.

Boats

Loos on ships are called 'the heads'. Traditionally, sailors pooped straight into the sea, hanging their bums over the side of the bow — the head of the vessel. This was the best place, because it was downwind and the bow wave washed the poop away.

Shockingly, modern cruise ships, some the size of floating towns, still discharge the untreated waste from their toilets into the sea. A cruise ship with 3,000 passengers can dump 1.3 million litres of sewage a week. Don't go swimming near one!

Trains

Until the 1880s, most railway carriages didn't have loos. Passengers had to cross their legs until the

train pulled into a station. Regular travellers bought urinals — ingenious rubber bladders that they strapped to their legs. They could wee into these under their clothes without anyone knowing (unless they leaked).

Train loos emptied straight onto the tracks until the 1980s. Signs asked passengers not to use the loo while the train was in a station — for obvious reasons. Modern trains have waste retention tanks that are emptied between journeys.

Leg strap

Rubber bladder

The wee collects in here

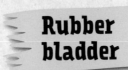

A GLANCE DOWN THE PAN
Space loos

Astronauts have to poo in **zero gravity**. Think about it – that means that everything floats: the astronaut, the stream of wee and even the **biggest poo**. To solve this problem, space toilets have foot restraints and a bar, like a rollercoaster safety bar, to pull across your thighs. The poo and wee are flushed with a stream of air.

Ah, the good old type 4 - textbook!

Poo meteorite
On the International Space Station, the wee is recycled into drinking water and the poo is packed into a capsule and fired into the Earth's atmosphere, where, luckily, it burns up. Imagine being hit by a superheated poo meteorite!

The Future of the Loo and all that Poo

Some use bushes...

So, we're agreed: Loos are important; so important that 19th November is World Toilet Day. This is a campaign to highlight huge hygiene problems around the world.

Loo witness

More than one billion people around the world have nowhere to poo. They use fields and bushes, ditches or railway tracks, or simply a plastic bag. To raise awareness, supporters of World Toilet Day stage publicity or fundraising events every year with a 'squat-in'! Everyone squats down on the ground and pretends to poo, which is a humorous way of highlighting a serious problem and helps raise funds for the cause.

Poo to the rescue

Scientists don't think western sewage systems are the answer for the developing world, especially where

A GLANCE DOWN THE PAN

Future loos

High tech The Bill Gates Foundation is backing a super loo designed by the California Institute of Technology. This is a flush toilet that uses the sun to power an electro-chemical reactor. This breaks down the waste into clean water and hydrogen gas. The gas is used to power the toilet at night, while the water can be reused to flush the toilet or to irrigate crops.

Low tech So simple, it's ingenious: biodegradable toilet bags. People poo into them and then bury the bags in a field. The soil helps to 'clean up' bacteria in the poo, so that it can fertilise crops safely.

water is scarce. But the problem is urgent – raw sewage from megacities has already poisoned thousands of kilometres of rivers and created dead zones across 250,000 square kilometres of ocean.

So it's time to look again at an old idea: putting human waste on crops. You produce 500 litres of wee and 50 kilograms of poop a year (OK, a grown man does, so your dad, your uncle...). Crucially, this contains around 10 kilograms of nitrogen, phosphorus and potassium – in just the right proportion to fertilise plants. The risks of spreading disease are pretty low. Urine is usually germ free, and if the faeces dry for a few months, dangerous pathogens die.

In some places, this is already happening. Bangalore in India has more than one million cesspits emptied by trucks called 'honey suckers'. The 'honey' is sold cheaply or given to local farmers. They save money on chemical fertiliser, and can still boost food production.

Glossary

Acropolis: main strongpoint of the city of Athens

bile: fluid that helps digest food

Bill Gates Foundation: Bill Gates is the billionaire founder of Microsoft. The Foundation is his charity dedicated to saving lives around the world with vaccination and sanitation programmes.

Black Death: bubonic plague that wiped out around one in three people in Europe during the fourteenth century

cesspit: storage pit for wee and poo

coprolite: fossilised poo

DNA: molecules that transmit information about how a living thing will look and function

gongfermors: workers who cleared drains, middens and cesspits

hip bath: shallow, short bath

lesions of the skin: skin problems including ulcers, scars and pustules

irrigation canals: trenches to take water from a source, such as a river, to crop fields

medieval: the Middle Ages – roughly 1000–1500 CE

megacities: cities of more than 10 million people

midden: pile of poo

migrants: people moving from one place to another, for example from the countryside to the cities

offal: intestines of dead animals, often used for food

parasite: an organism which survives by living in or on another living being

pathogens: microorganisms that can cause disease

pharmacology: the study of drugs

piss pot: medieval jar to wee in

poultice: a dressing for an injury

quicklime: a powder made from limestone that can be used as a disinfectant

rehydrated: liquid put back into something dry

saltpetre: potassium nitrate; used to make gunpowder

sanitation: providing people with clean drinking water and sewage disposal

scribe: scholar and trained writer

stalls: toilet cubicles

urinate: have a wee

water closets: WCs or flush toilets

More information

 ## Places to visit

(apart from your own toilet, of course)

Gladstone Pottery Museum in Stoke-on-Trent, Staffordshire
The museum hosts a permanent 'Flushed with Pride' exhibition to celebrate the region's significant role in toilet manufacturing. http://www.stokemuseums.org.uk/visit/gpm/

Museum of Science and Industry, Manchester Walk through a Victorian sewer in the Underground Manchester Gallery. http://www.mosi.org.uk/

Blists Hill Victorian Town, Shropshire Tour the town and look for the Victorian loos. http://www.ironbridge.org.uk/

Housesteads Roman Fort One of the best sets of surviving loos of the Roman Empire. http://www.english-heritage.org.uk/daysout/properties/housesteads-roman-fort-hadrians-wall/

 ## Websites

http://www.wateraid.org/uk/get-involved/world-toilet-day
This site looks at the problems of toilets in developing countries today.

http://www.show.me.uk/site/news/ST01206.html
Read all about toilets through the ages on this fun site.

 ## Books

Truth or Busted: Medieval People Washed their Clothes in Wee!
by Kay Barnham, Wayland (2012)

Poop Happened by Sarah Albee, Walker (2010)

Poo! A History of the World from the Bottom Up! by Sarah Albee, A&C Black (2012)

Don't Flush! Lifting the Lid on the Science of Poo and Wee
by Richard and Mary Platt, Kingfisher (2012)

Index

MORE HISTORY THAN YOU CAN SHAKE A STICK AT!

Why not find out more about the terrible Tudors, dastardly dictators and the raucous Romans with our array of humorous history titles...

TRUTH or BUSTED

WORLD WAR ONE MADE SOLDIERS' FEET GO ROTTEN!

The fact or fiction behind **BATTLES & WARS**

978 0 7502 8132 4

TRUTH or BUSTED

MEDIEVAL PEOPLE WASHED THEIR CLOTHES IN WEE!

Weeee!

The fact or fiction behind **HISTORY**

978 0 7502 6958 2

TRUTH or BUSTED

HENRY VIII BUILT A 14-SEAT LAVATORY!

The fact or fiction behind **TUDORS**

978 0 7502 8130 0

TRUTH or BUSTED

VICTORIAN WORKERS TURNED DOG POO INTO GOLD!

The fact or fiction behind **VICTORIANS**

978 0 7502 8129 4

TRUTH or BUSTED

FEMALE PHARAOHS WORE FALSE BEARDS!

The fact or fiction behind **EGYPTIANS**

978 0 7502 8133 1

TRUTH or BUSTED

WARM GLADIATOR BLOOD WAS USED AS MEDICINE!

The fact or fiction behind **ROMANS**

978 0 7502 8134 8

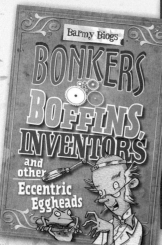

Barmy Biogs

BONKERS BOFFINS, INVENTORS and other Eccentric Eggheads

978 0 7502 7718 1

Barmy Biogs

CRACKPOT KINGS, QUEENS and other Daft Royals

978 0 7502 7717 4

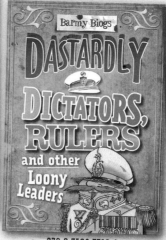

Barmy Biogs

DASTARDLY DICTATORS, RULERS and other Loony Leaders

978 0 7502 7720 4

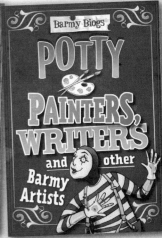

Barmy Biogs

POTTY PAINTERS, WRITERS and other Barmy Artists

978 0 7502 7719 8